MYSTERY HUNTERS

TOMBS AND CURSED TREASURE

Robyn Hardyman

Gareth Stevens PUBLISHING

Please visit our website, www.garethstevens.com.
For a free color catalog of all our high-quality books,
call toll free 1-800-542-2595 of fax 1-877-542-2596.

Cataloging-in-Publication Data

Names: Hardyman, Robyn.
Title: Tombs and cursed treasure / Robyn Hardyman.
Description: New York : Gareth Stevens, 2017. | Series: Mystery hunters | Includes index.
Identifiers: ISBN 9781482460117 (pbk.) | ISBN 9781482460131 (library bound) |
ISBN 9781482460124 (6 pack)
Subjects: LCSH: Tombs--Juvenile literature. | Excavations (Archaeology)--Juvenile literature. |
Classification: LCC CC77.B8 H349 2017 | DDC 930.1--dc23

First Edition

Published in 2017 by
Gareth Stevens Publishing
111 East 14th Street, Suite 349
New York, NY 10003

Produced for Gareth Stevens by Calcium
Editors: Sarah Eason and Claudia Martin
Picture researcher: Rachel Blount
Designer: Emma DeBanks

Picture credits: Cover: Shutterstock: Everett – Art bl, Pakhnyushchy c, Eduardo Rivero tr; Inside: NOAA: Institute for Exploration/University of Rhode Island or NOAA/IFE/URI 31b; Shutterstock: Airphoto.gr 9t, Anton_Ivanov16–17bg, Dray van Beeck 30–31bg, Jason Benz Bennee 12–13bg, Andrey Burmakin 22b, Rafal Cichawa 24t, Pichugin Dmitry 22–23bg, Everett – Art 10b, 11t, 21t, 29t, 42c, Everett Historical 31t, 38t, Fat Jackey 36–37bg, Dean Fikar 38–39bg, Iakov Filimonov 4b, Fotoluminate LLC 39t, Filip Fuxa 40–41bg, Leonardo Gonzalez 5, Jaroslaw Grudzinski 42–43bg, David Hughes 20–21bg, Humannet 14–15bg, Ammit Jack 6–7bg, Javarman 28b, Worapan Kong 18–19bg, Steve Lovegrove 25r, Maodoltee 24–25 bg, Marco_tb 8b, Myotis 35b, Nejron Photo 32–33bg, Petersemler-photography 37t, Pushish Images 4–5bg, Eduardo Rivero 1, Vaughan Sam 8–9bg, Carlos E. Santa Maria 7t, Antonio S 34t, Sculpies 12b, Denis Tabler 34–35bg, VojtechVlk 28–29bg, WaitForLight 16b, Xbrchx 41b, Yaping 18t, Yeko Photo Studio 33b; Wikimedia Commons: 14b, 15t, Osama Shukir Muhammed Amin FRCP(Glasg) 26t, Brooklyn Museum 6t, Imagen fotografiada y subida por Discjockey 40b, SAC Andy Holmes (RAF) 26–27bg, Illuminated manuscript, De Rege Johanne, 1300-1400. MS Cott. Claud DII, folio 116, British Library 36b, Mathae (Stipich Béla) 20b, Richard McCully 42–43t, R.F.Morgan 13t, Francisco Rodrigues 32t, U0045269 27b, Unknown / (of the reproduction) Staatsbibliothek Berlin/Schacht 23t, Wit 17, Zcm11 19t.

Printed in China

CPSIA compliance information: Batch #CW17GS: For further information contact Gareth Stevens, New York, New York at 1-800-542-2595.

CONTENTS

Chapter 1

TALES OF TREASURE

For centuries, tales of lost treasure have excited and dazzled us. Many legends tell of deadly curses linked with hoards of lost treasure. Despite these warnings, adventurers set out on dangerous quests to find treasures buried in the desert or lost beneath the ocean waves. Some do not return home. Many books and movies are based on these mysteries. But sometimes the truth can be even stranger, and more terrifying, than fiction.

Riches for the Next Life

There is something really exciting about the idea of a lost tomb, a hidden place of burial for someone who was famous—and probably wealthy, too. Were they buried with many precious goods? History is full of stories of lost tombs and hidden treasure. Emperors, kings, **pharaohs**, and rulers of all kinds are said to have taken with them to the grave the riches they **amassed** during their lives. Often, this was because of their beliefs about the **afterlife**. If they were going to be living a new kind of life after death, they would need their belongings with them. Some rulers have even been buried with mini kitchens and cooking equipment! Others had just their most precious things. In this book, we will explore the best mysteries of lost tombs, and we will unearth some fantastic treasure.

Stories of cursed treasure have fascinated people for centuries!

Lost at Sea

Sometimes treasure is lost in other ways. It may not be buried with its dead owner; it may simply disappear. Perhaps we have written records describing it, but as the treasure has never been found we cannot know if the records are true. Over the centuries, a great burial place for treasure has been the ocean. As ships sailed across the seas, carrying valuable goods to trade with other nations, they were often sunk by storms or attacked by their enemies. It can be very difficult to locate these treasure hoards and bring them to the surface, but many, many people have risked their lives to do so.

This wrecked ship is now home to schools of fish. If it once carried treasure, it is lost to the waves.

MYSTERY HUNTER

Look for the Mystery Hunter boxes throughout the book. They will ask you to look at the information given in each chapter and answer questions based on what you have read. Then turn to pages 44–45 to see if your answer is correct.

As ruler of the Inca, Atahualpa was treated almost as a god.

The Lost Gold of Atahualpa

The Inca controlled a huge **empire** in western South America from the middle of the fifteenth century. Their lands stretched over more than 2,000 miles (3,200 km) and they ruled up to 8 million people, from different groups and with different languages. Their emperor was called the Sapa Inca, and he was treated almost as a god. In 1532, the emperor was Atahualpa (c. 1500–1533). He had just gained the right to rule by winning a five-year battle with his brother, which had weakened the empire. It was then that the Spanish **conquistador** Francisco Pizarro (1471/6–1541) arrived with his men.

One important source of Inca wealth was gold. The Spanish knew this, and were determined to get their hands on it. Pizarro and his men seized Atahualpa and took him prisoner. Atahualpa promised the Spanish a huge hoard of gold, enough to fill a whole room, if they would let him go. The Inca gathered the treasure, and the Spanish are said to have taken some of it, but then they killed Atahualpa anyway. The question is, what happened to the rest of the treasure?

Cursed Treasure?

The legend says that the treasure was buried by an Inca general somewhere in the Llanganates Mountains in Ecuador. Ever since, the search for the Inca gold has been one of the greatest treasure hunts in history. Several treasure hunters have died in their attempts. About 50 years after Atahualpa's death, a Spaniard named Valverde apparently found the treasure. He left directions to its location before he died. Many people have tried to follow these directions, and in 1886 one person is reported to have found the treasure, but he died on his way home.

This amazing gold mask is the kind of treasure that might be buried with Atahualpa.

Then, in 2013, an international team of **archaeologists** found a curious site in the Llanganates Mountains. It was a tall, sloping stone structure with a flat top, hidden by trees and bushes. Could this be the place where Atahualpa lies buried, along with his treasure? The site is still waiting to be fully explored.

MYSTERY HUNTER

Considering the information you have read, do you think that Atahualpa's treasure is still hidden somewhere? Could it have survived all this time without anyone finding it? Would the Inca have buried it out of sight? Give reasons for your answers.

Is Atahualpa's treasure somewhere in the Llanganates Mountains of Ecuador?

Chapter 2

MYSTERIES OF ANCIENT EGYPT

The people of ancient Egypt formed an extraordinary civilization about 5,000 years ago. Their culture endured for almost 3,000 years. Their building skills were so advanced that many of their temples and pyramids are still standing today. These buildings have always fascinated archaeologists, and over the past few hundred years many discoveries have been made about them. But are there more secrets waiting to be revealed?

Flooding sealed the tomb of the valley's most famous pharaoh, Tutankhamun (c. 1341–1323 BC), so tomb robbers did not find it.

Valley of the Kings

Until 1500 BC, the Egyptian pharaohs were buried in great pyramid tombs. Then, from 1550 BC to 1070 BC, Egyptian rulers were buried in underground tombs in a valley known as the Valley of the Kings. More than 60 tombs have been identified there. Some are small, while others are very elaborate, with many **chambers**. Most of the tombs were robbed hundreds or even thousands of years ago. But not every royal person from that period has been accounted for. There are some whose tombs we have not found. Could they still be **intact** somewhere?

Between 2007 and 2010, archaeologists made the most thorough exploration of the area since the 1920s. They used techniques that would not damage the tombs or their contents, such as **radar** scanners. Radar scanners send radio waves into the ground. These bounce off different materials in different ways, creating an image of what lies beneath the surface. What the archaeologists found got everyone excited. They think there are several small hidden tombs that no one can have reached to rob. There is possibly a big tomb, too, which must have belonged to a very important person. It will take a long time to analyze all the findings, but the whole world would be excited to find a new pharaoh's tomb!

*This tomb painting has figures of gods and **hieroglyphic** writing.*

The Valley of the Kings is on the west bank of the Nile River in Egypt.

MYSTERIOUS FACTS

Egyptian tombs contain valuable **evidence** about the people buried there:

- Tombs hold records of the dead person's life, in the form of pictures and writing. These were painted and written on the walls and on scrolls made of a kind of paper called papyrus.
- The Egyptians' writing was called hieroglyphics. It uses pictures as symbols to represent letters and whole words.

Tutankhamun's solid gold death mask is topped by a cobra. This represents the goddess Wadjet, protector of the pharaohs.

Curse of the Pharaohs

The most famous tomb in the Valley of the Kings is that of the pharaoh Tutankhamun, who was buried around 3,300 years ago. The tomb was found in 1922 by British archaeologist Howard Carter (1874–1939). When Carter and his team opened the tomb, they discovered fabulous treasure. The pharaoh's coffin was solid gold. Next to him was his throne and an array of other treasures, all things the pharaoh would need in the afterlife. But was the glittering treasure cursed?

Were Carter and his team cursed when they opened Pharaoh Tutankhamun's glorious tomb?

The Legend

Legend has it that anyone who disturbs an ancient Egyptian mummy will be cursed. This is known as the "Curse of the Pharaohs." The evidence for this curse is in a couple of **inscriptions** on tombs, promising punishment to anyone who dares enter. Perhaps the inscriptions were intended to warn away tomb robbers. However, there is no such inscription on the tomb of Tutankhamun. No one really talked about the Curse of the Pharaohs until the strange case of Howard Carter and his team.

Terrible Deaths

Howard Carter was not alone when he opened Tutankhamun's tomb: he was surrounded by workers as well as Lord George Carnarvon, who was paying for the expedition. A few days later, Carter's canary was killed by a cobra. The cobra, symbol of the Egyptian goddess Wadjet, is said to be the protector of pharaohs. Rumors began that the tomb was cursed. Four months later, Lord Carnarvon died from blood poisoning caused by a mosquito bite. A month after that, a visitor to the tomb, George Jay Gould I, died from a fever. The following year, Sir Archibald Douglas-Reid, who had X-rayed Tutankhamun's mummy, died. The list goes on... Within eight years of opening the tomb, a total of 10 people connected with it were dead. Howard Carter died of cancer in 1939.

Was the tomb really cursed, or were the deaths just coincidences? In the 1920s, it was not as easy to treat illnesses such as blood poisoning and fevers as it is today. In the days before vaccinations, it was common for travelers to fall sick. Perhaps we will never know the truth.

Secrets of the Pyramids

The Valley of the Kings is not the only site in ancient Egypt that is causing great excitement among archaeologists. The most famous monuments from this ancient civilization are the magnificent pyramids at Giza, near modern Cairo. Could it be that the pyramids, too, are about to reveal great secrets—secrets that they have kept hidden for thousands of years?

The Great Pyramid

The Great Pyramid at Giza was completed in about 2560 BC, after 20 years' work. It was designed to be the tomb for a pharaoh named Khufu. Alongside it are two more pyramids, for the pharaohs Khafre and Menkaure. Inside the Great Pyramid, three main rooms were found by early explorers: the king's chamber, the queen's chamber, and the grand gallery. None contained treasure, as it had probably been stolen by tomb robbers hundreds of years before. Experts have always wondered if there could be more chambers and tunnels inside the massive structure. They want to understand more about how the pyramids were built, and they want them to give up their secrets!

Could new secrets be revealed at the Pyramids of Giza?

This is an internal plan of the Great Pyramid. What secrets might still lie inside it?

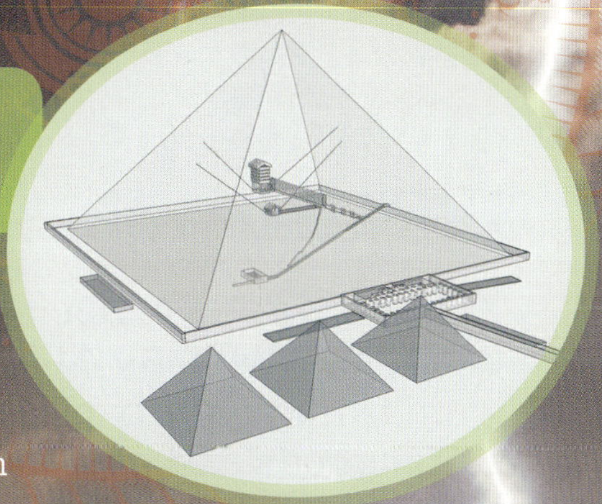

In 2016, **thermal** scans of the Great Pyramid revealed something exciting. These scans can detect differences in temperature. There seemed to be unusual temperature differences on both the eastern side and the northern side of the pyramid. These suggested there might be open spaces inside. The archaeologists planned to continue the scans over a longer time period in order to rule out the results being affected by factors such as the air temperature or the wind.

The Red Pyramid

The same technology has been used to scan another Egyptian pyramid, the Red Pyramid at Dahshur, a few miles away from Giza. Here, the researchers have found a difference in temperature between the top and the bottom, but only on one side. It will be a tense wait to see what this might mean, but this amazing ability to "see" inside solid rock constructions is certainly helping us solve the mysteries of these wonderful places.

MYSTERY HUNTER

Considering what you have read in this chapter, do you think the "Curse of the Pharaohs" really exists? Give reasons for your answer.

Chapter 3

RICHES OF ANCIENT CHINA

The civilization of ancient China was one of the world's earliest. By 4,000 years ago, Chinese kings were ruling orderly cities where craftspeople created metal goods and pottery. At its largest, the Chinese empire was enormous, and its rulers were extremely powerful. The ancient Chinese invented many things we still use today, such as paper and tea as a drink. This important civilization is full of puzzles.

Mystery Identity

Sometimes, historians know about a figure from the past but the location of his or her burial remains a mystery. Perhaps a tomb is found, but getting access to it is difficult. A different kind of mystery arises when archaeologists find a tomb but do not know to whom it belongs. The work then begins to piece together the puzzle of its occupant.

This is the case with a remarkable tomb **complex** found in the province of Jiangxi in southern China in 2015. The tomb dates back 2,000 years and is in very good condition, so it is of great historical importance. Several people are buried there. Could they have been members of a ruling family? So far, a hoard of more than 20,000 objects has been found there. These include gold bars and plates, copper coins, and other precious goods.

The Jiangxi tomb riches suggest an important person was buried there.

Some of the gold bars are inscribed with the ancient Chinese characters for "up," "middle," and "down." What could these mean?

Unlucky Emperor

The most likely explanation the experts have is that this is the tomb of an emperor who had one of the shortest reigns in history. Liu He (c. 92–59 BC) ruled for just 27 days before he was forced from the throne and banished to the south of China. By comparing the found objects with other ancient sources, archaeologists are trying to solve this mystery of identity.

These beautiful bronze statues were among the treasures in the tomb.

MYSTERIOUS FACTS

Consider this list of some of the objects found in the mysterious tomb:

- Buried in the tomb are nearly 3,000 bamboo strips used to keep records. Experts are trying to figure out what their ancient script means.
- A portrait of the Chinese **philosopher** Confucius (551–479 BC) was found in the tomb. It is one of the earliest known images of this famous figure.
- Some of the solid gold bars in the tomb are shaped like horses' hooves.

The First Emperor

The first emperor of China was Qin Shi Huang (260–210 BC). His father was king of one of the seven states in China, called Qin. The states were constantly fighting each other, but when Huang took over from his father he conquered all the others. In 221 BC, he declared himself emperor of all China. He was the first emperor of the Qin **dynasty**.

Qin Shi Huang ruled with a firm hand and expected all the different peoples in his empire to obey the laws he laid down. He must also have wanted people to remember him long after his death, because he ordered 700,000 workers to build him a remarkably impressive tomb complex. He ordered a huge army of clay soldiers to be buried with him.

These are just a few of the 8,000 clay soldiers protecting the tomb.

A Hidden Tomb

Qin Shi Huang's remarkable tomb complex was discovered only in 1974, by farmers digging a well. What they found became headline news around the world. In a huge pit, each one of the 8,000 clay soldiers has a unique face, formed by the hands of skilled craftspeople to look like individuals. With them are horses and chariots. This army was meant to protect the emperor in the afterlife. But this is not the end of the story. The main tomb, containing the body of Qin Shi Huang, remains unopened. Archaeologists believe the entire tomb complex measures 3.9 miles (6.3 km) around its outer edge. The complex was modeled on the emperor's real capital city. One ancient source says it contains "palaces and scenic towers for 100 officials," as well as a hoard of rare treasures.

The emperor's main tomb remains hidden beneath this mound.

Rivers of Poison

The main tomb has been located but not opened. It was never going to be easy to get inside this mysterious tomb. Its builders were apparently told to make traps that would fire arrows at anyone trying to enter. **Probes** inserted by archaeologists reveal there are rivers of a poisonous metal called mercury running around it underground. To ensure that the secrets of the tomb's contents could never be shared, all the builders were sealed inside, to die alongside the emperor. Today, archaeologists are trying to unlock the tomb's secrets, but they must be careful not to release mercury into the streams nearby. This would be a disastrous curse for local people. For now, we can only imagine the riches that lie within the tomb.

Ancient Chinese coins had square holes drilled through the center, so they could be held on chains or cords.

Liu Fei's Great Tomb

Qin Shi Huang is not the only Chinese ruler whose burial was shrouded in mystery. Liu Fei (169–128 BC) was prince of the kingdom of Jiangdu during the reign of a dynasty called the Han. He was the son of Emperor Jing and the half-brother of Emperor Wu. He was buried in an elaborate tomb that befitted his high status, but this burial place lay hidden away for more than 2,000 years.

The tomb was found in 2009, when engineers looking for a site to build a new **quarry** called in archaeologists to check the location they chose. Unlike with Qin Shi Huang's tomb, we have been able to make more progress in solving the puzzle. When the tomb was opened, it revealed the kind of treasure hoard that most archaeologists only dream of. Archaeologists found a tomb complex containing three major tombs, eleven smaller ones, two pits full of weapons, and two pits for horses and chariots that contain horse skeletons.

This is the kind of jade suit that Chinese rulers were dressed in for burial.

Treasure Hoard

Although Liu Fei's body was missing, presumably stolen hundreds of years ago, what was left behind was enough to fill several museums. There were more than 10,000 objects: gold, silver, and bronze vessels; weapons; lamps; bowls; and even musical instruments. A treasury contained more than 100,000 coins. Around the place where Liu would have been lying were fragments of a very special burial suit. The Chinese buried their important figures in suits made of hundreds of small pieces of a rare and precious green stone called jade. The pieces were connected with metal threads.

As if this extraordinary hoard were not enough, in one of the smaller tombs, archaeologists found something even more exceptional. This was an entire coffin made of jade. This is the only jade coffin known to have survived in Chinese history.

MYSTERY HUNTER

Do you think it will ever be possible to unlock the secrets of Qin Shi Huang's tomb? Are the traps of weapons and poisons laid by this cunning emperor enough to keep us out forever? Justify your answers with information you have read in this chapter.

Chapter 4

WHERE ARE THEY BURIED?

When people are buried, it is usual for their loved ones to put up a stone or some other sign to mark the location of the grave. Throughout history, however, some people have been buried in unmarked graves. Sometimes the circumstances of their death made it impossible to mark the spot, such as in wartime. At other times, the marker has disappeared over time and we do not know the location of the grave. When the person who died is important, mystery hunters want to find the grave—and maybe even find treasure, too.

King Midas

In the ancient Greek legend, King Midas of Phrygia was a tragic figure. He had the power to turn everything he touched to gold. How wonderful, you might think! But it was really a curse: it meant that anything he touched, even his loved ones, became solid gold and died. There was a real king, Mydos, who ruled in Phrygia in about 710 BC. In 1957, archaeologists found a burial mound containing the skeleton of a man in the region of Turkey that was once Phrygia. Could this be the burial place of the king? The dates of the pottery and other **artifacts** found inside the tomb suggest it could be, but no hoard of gold was discovered.

Could this burial mound belong to the legendary King Midas of Phrygia?

A Simple End

Kings do not always have lavish burials. King Henry VIII (1491–1547) was one of the most famous rulers in English history, yet he has no elaborate tomb to commemorate him. He planned for a great monument to be built, but in the end he wanted to be buried beside his favorite wife, Jane Seymour (c. 1508–1537). His body was stored in a **vault** under the floor of the chapel of a royal residence, Windsor Castle, next to hers, until his own monument could be finished. But it never was, and the project was forgotten. The vault was briefly opened up to hold the body of King Charles I (1600–1649), who was executed during the English Civil War. The vault was forgotten until 1813, when it was rediscovered by workmen. Today, a simple slab on the floor marks the place where all three bodies lie.

Henry VIII's burial site was forgotten for hundreds of years.

Windsor Castle in England is the burial place for many British kings and queens.

Genghis Khan

Many centuries ago, Genghis Khan (c. 1162–1227) founded the huge Mongol empire. Khan means "ruler." At its greatest, the empire stretched from China in the east to eastern Europe in the west. It was the largest empire the world had ever seen. Mysteriously, no one knows for sure where this great leader is buried. This great puzzle of history has remained unsolved for 800 years.

A Secret Grave

At first, the Mongols were **nomadic** people. They moved from place to place on horseback across the plains of Central Asia. There were many Mongol tribes, but one man, Genghis Khan, united them in about AD 1206. He was a brilliant leader and warrior, and led his army in conquest after conquest. When he died in 1227, he gave instructions that the place of his burial should remain secret. The soldiers carrying his body killed anyone they met and also killed the slaves who built his underground tomb. After they had buried Genghis Khan, the soldiers killed themselves.

This modern statue honors the great leader Genghis Khan.

There are several theories about where the grave may be. All the theories agree that Genghis lies in Mongolia, his homeland. One source suggests a river was diverted to run over the grave, to hide it. Another says that 10,000 horses stampeded over it to flatten the mound. Genghis would have been buried with many precious goods, as well as horses and probably other people, to keep him company.

The Mongols were feared warriors and excellent riders.

A High Place

One thing we do know is that it was Mongol **custom** to bury important people on high ground. The location that historians think is most likely for Genghis's grave is a holy mountain called Burkhan Khaldun. This land has always been protected by the Mongolians: no outsiders have been allowed to enter it. Ancient sources say Genghis went there for refuge when he was young, so it must have been important to him. This location also fits in with historical accounts of the burial, which say it took place in a location where three rivers meet.

Can the top of this mountain be **excavated**? Not at the moment. Many Mongolians believe it is forbidden to disturb a grave. Anyone who did so would be cursed. An international team has recently begun scanning the area with radar, to see if this mountain can offer up its secrets.

Was Genghis Khan buried on Burkhan Khaldun mountain?

Tu Dúc enjoyed boating on the lake and sitting in the ***pavilion****, but where was he buried?*

Tu Dúc and His Plans

Turning the clock forward a few hundred years, we come to another Asian ruler with a serious determination to keep his burial place a secret. This was Tu Dúc (1829–1883), the ruler of the Nguyen empire in Vietnam. He ruled for longer than any other emperor of the Nguyen dynasty, from 1848 to 1883. He was anxious to have a son to succeed him, but although he had more than 100 wives, none of them ever bore him a child. So his thoughts turned to leaving a **legacy** of a different kind. He made elaborate plans for his burial and tomb.

There is no mystery about where the tomb complex is. It is in Hué, the capital of the empire. Most of the buildings were completed before Tu Dúc died, and he enjoyed using them. There was a lake for boating and a pavilion to sit in and admire the view. There was also a grand tomb monument, ready and waiting. All was set for a glorious royal burial when the emperor died. So where is the mystery?

Not There

The mystery is that Tu Dúc had other plans. He had this elaborate burial complex built, but he was never buried there. Instead he planned his burial for a different location—one that remains a secret to this day. Tu Dúc did not curse his treasure but he certainly cursed his laborers: to make sure his secret would not come out, he arranged for the laborers who buried him to be killed after they had finished.

It is widely thought that the real tomb is somewhere near Hué. Some think it may be on the island in the middle of the lake in the tomb complex. Others say it is well away from this complex, to keep its secret forever.

The fake tomb is guarded by statues of attendants.

MYSTERIOUS FACTS

Consider these facts about Tu Dúc's fake tomb complex:

- The tomb complex took three long years to build and includes dozens of buildings.
- Tu Dúc wrote a long story all about his life, carved on a large stone column called a stele. It stands near his fake tomb.

King Gilgamesh

The story of Gilgamesh was carved in clay tablets in a kind of writing called ***cuneiform***.

The story of King Gilgamesh is one of the oldest ever written down. It was carved onto a set of clay tablets more than 4,500 years ago. It tells the story of the life of Gilgamesh, who was said to be a king of the city of Uruk, in ancient Mesopotamia in the Middle East. This is the city from which modern Iraq gets its name. Many historians think Gilgamesh was more than just a story and that he actually existed, ruling Uruk some time between about 2800 and 2500 BC. A small part of the great city of Uruk was excavated by archaeologists in the nineteenth century. However, the location of the last resting place of Gilgamesh has remained a mystery for thousands of years. Could it finally have been found? Does it even exist?

Buried Beneath a River

The story goes that Gilgamesh was a man of superhuman strength. He built up the walls of the city of Uruk to defend his people. During his life he had many adventures, and at the end he was buried under the Euphrates River. How was this possible? The story says that the waters of the great river parted after his death so he could be buried somewhere he would never be disturbed.

These excavations have uncovered buildings that were part of the large city of Uruk, in the desert of Iraq.

A City Revealed

In 2003, an international team of archaeologists began exploring the area of Uruk. They researched where the Euphrates River used to run in ancient times, and used scanners that can tell the difference in the ground between ordinary earth and mud bricks used for construction. As they worked, the archaeologists were amazed to find that Uruk's entire town plan started to emerge! They found places described in the story of Gilgamesh, such as gardens and a complex system of canals. Most exciting of all, in the middle of where the river used to flow lay the remains of a building that could have been a burial place. Surely this must belong to Gilgamesh? War and violence in the region has made it difficult to continue the work, but the possibilities for future investigation are exciting.

The all-powerful Gilgamesh is said to have wrestled a bull.

Kings of the Aztec

The Aztec empire flourished from the fourteenth to the sixteenth centuries in lands that today are in Mexico. The Aztec ruled over many different groups of people, each with their own city-state, but the empire's capital city, Tenochtitlán, was truly magnificent. At the head of this great empire was the king. The people believed he was chosen to rule by the gods, and that he was all-powerful.

City of Tenochtitlán

At the height of the Aztec empire, 200,000 people may have been living in Tenochtitlán. The city was located on an island in the middle of a lake, and included gardens, towers, and canals. At its heart was an enormous **sacred** area, surrounded by a wall. Inside were stepped pyramids, called **ziggurats**. On the flat top of the largest, the Great Temple, were shrines to the war god and the rain god. Human sacrifice was an important part of Aztec worship, so thousands of people were killed here each year. However, although we know a great deal about Aztec religious practices, we know very little about how and where they buried their kings. Could this be about to change?

The remains of the Great Temple of Tenochtitlán are in the center of modern Mexico City.

This nineteenth-century painting shows the great King Moctezuma I receiving a messenger.

Hidden Chambers

Today, the ruins of the Great Temple of Tenochtitlán lie among the modern streets of Mexico City. Archaeologists have recently made some thrilling discoveries there that might solve the mystery of the tombs of the Aztec kings. They came across a hidden tunnel and a secret passageway leading to a round structure. This is very similar to the chambers that the records say were used to burn the bodies of important people. Remarkably, there are also two sealed doorways. Could kings be buried inside? Could they have been buried with hoards of treasure?

These possible tombs date from the height of the Aztec empire. One could belong to the great King Moctezuma I (c. 1398–1469), who greatly expanded the empire. In 1519, the Spanish conquistador Hernán Cortés (1485–1547) arrived in Tenochtitlán. He took King Moctezuma II (c. 1466–1520) prisoner, and the Aztec empire soon came to an end. We will have to wait a little longer to find out if this mystery can finally be solved, as the archaeologists have yet to open the sealed chambers…

MYSTERY HUNTER

Based on what you have read about Gilgamesh and the city of Uruk, do you think archaeologists have discovered the burial place of Gilgamesh in Iraq? Give reasons for your answer.

Chapter 5

SHIPWRECK

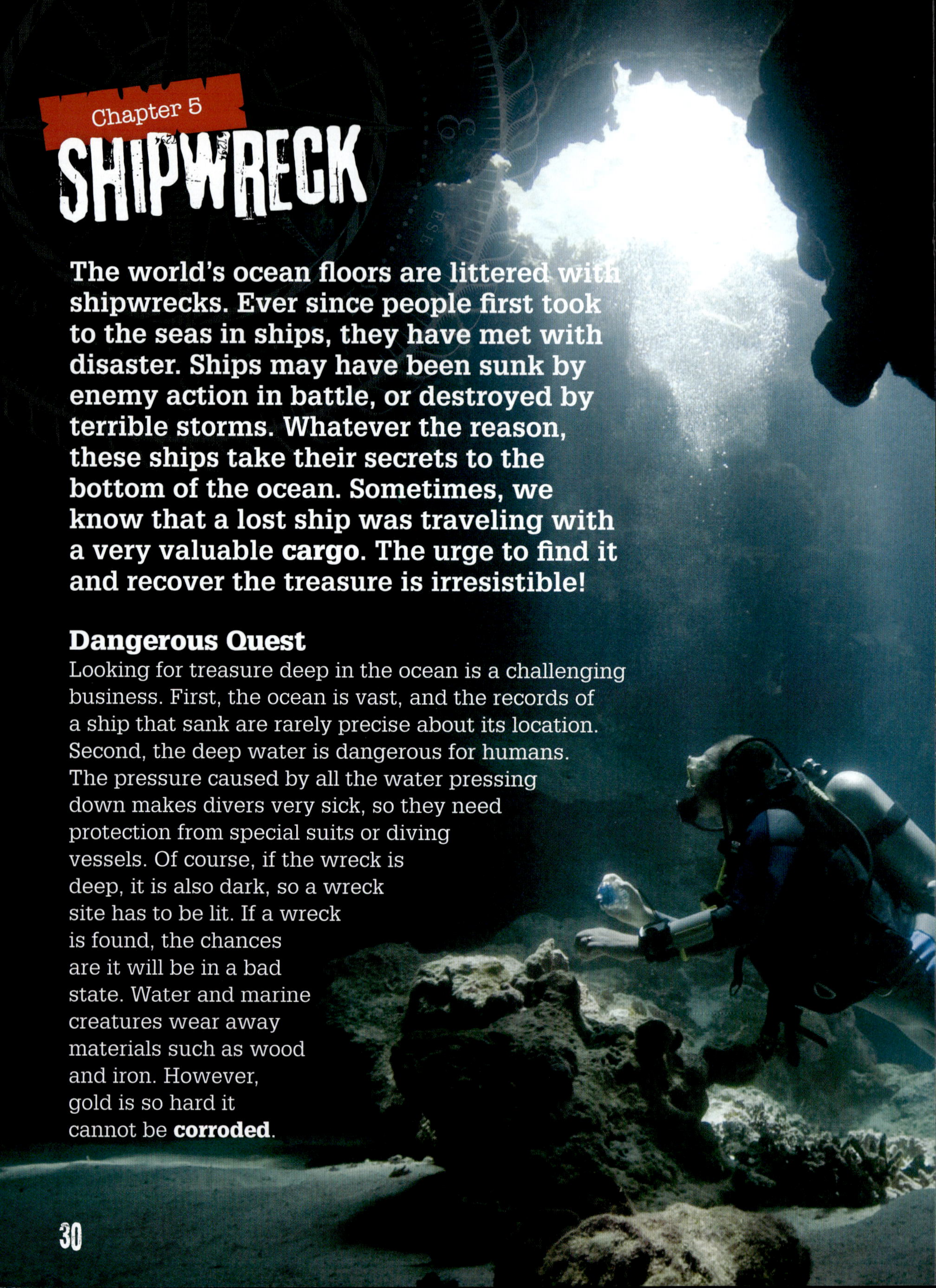

The world's ocean floors are littered with shipwrecks. Ever since people first took to the seas in ships, they have met with disaster. Ships may have been sunk by enemy action in battle, or destroyed by terrible storms. Whatever the reason, these ships take their secrets to the bottom of the ocean. Sometimes, we know that a lost ship was traveling with a very valuable cargo. The urge to find it and recover the treasure is irresistible!

Dangerous Quest

Looking for treasure deep in the ocean is a challenging business. First, the ocean is vast, and the records of a ship that sank are rarely precise about its location. Second, the deep water is dangerous for humans. The pressure caused by all the water pressing down makes divers very sick, so they need protection from special suits or diving vessels. Of course, if the wreck is deep, it is also dark, so a wreck site has to be lit. If a wreck is found, the chances are it will be in a bad state. Water and marine creatures wear away materials such as wood and iron. However, gold is so hard it cannot be **corroded**.

Treasure Ships

Ships carried treasure for many reasons. From the fifteenth to the early twentieth centuries, many nations were exploring the world by sea and building empires. The Spaniards, for example, loaded their ships with gold from their **colonies** in the Americas to take back to Spain. Meanwhile, British ships carried goods from British-ruled India and other colonies to trade with the rest of the world.

Many passengers and crew died when the Titanic *sank in 1912.*

The *Titanic*

One of the most famous shipwrecks ever was of RMS *Titanic*, a huge passenger ship that sank in 1912 on its first crossing from Europe to the United States after it hit an iceberg. The wreck was finally located in 1985 by a team using a remotely controlled deep-sea vehicle with cameras. It lies 12,000 feet (3,700 m) below the surface of the Atlantic Ocean. Thousands of artifacts have been brought to the surface, including objects used by the crew and passengers. Although they are fascinating, they are not quite treasure as we think of it.

The bow of the Titanic *is thousands of feet underwater.*

The Flor do Mar *was lost to the sea.*

The *Flor do Mar*

In 1505, a Portuguese warship named the *Flor do Mar* (Flower of the Sea) set sail on a lengthy voyage. It was part of a group of ships setting off to India, far away to the east. Over the following years, the ship saw many battles and adventures. In 1511, it was involved in the conquest of Malacca, in modern Malaysia, where it collected a huge amount of treasure. The crew planned to take it home and present it to the king of Portugal. On the way back to Portugal, however, the ship sailed into a violent storm off the coast of the island of Sumatra, in modern Indonesia. This is an area of strong ocean **currents**. The *Flor do Mar* sank below the waves, with the loss of 400 men and one of the richest hoards of treasure ever collected.

MYSTERIOUS FACTS

In 1985, the wreck of the Spanish ship *Nuestra Señora de Atocha* was found by U.S. treasure hunter Mel Fisher. The ship had gone down in a storm off Florida in 1622. The treasure is worth $450 million.

Diamonds and Perfumes

Ever since, the *Flor do Mar* has been the ultimate prize for treasure hunters. There has been endless debate about where the ship lies, and many expeditions have set off in search of her riches. Men have wasted fortunes trying to solve this mystery. One U.S. treasure seeker was said to have spent $20 million in the search. Today, treasure hunters can use underwater vehicles equipped with cameras and sonar. Sonar is a system that sends out sound waves then waits for the waves to bounce off surrounding objects in order to build up a picture of the underwater environment.

Still, 500 years later, no one has found the sunken treasure. When someone does, the find will be spectacular. In 1511, Malacca was a large trading center, and the ship's crew collected many riches. One source described some of it: "She was also carrying four sitting lions made of gold with perfumes inside. They used to be in the chamber of the King of Malacca, their eyes, tongues, teeth, and nails were made of precious stones." The ship was also carrying precious gems and diamonds sent by the kingdom of Thailand as gifts for the king of Portugal. Both Portugal and Malaysia have claimed any treasure that is eventually found. The mystery of the *Flor do Mar* remains unsolved.

The Flor do Mar *was said to have been carrying 200 cases of diamonds and other precious stones.*

The San José *was a* ***galleon*** *like this one.*

The *San José*

Another ship that sank carrying a staggering cargo of treasure was the Spanish galleon *San José*. This ship sank off the coast of Colombia in June 1708. For over 300 years it has remained at the bottom of the ocean, one of the most amazing, and valuable, shipwrecks in history.

Spanish Treasure

The *San José* was part of a convoy of ships carrying treasure to King Philip V (1683–1746) of Spain. This was the time of the War of the Spanish Succession (1701–1714), a war between Spain, England, the Netherlands, France, and other nations over Philip's right to take the throne. The Spanish ship was taking a vast store of gold and other treasure back to Spain from its colonies in the Americas. In June 1708, the ill-fated ship met a fleet of English ships and an explosion on board sent it plummeting to the bottom of the Caribbean Sea, near the island of Baru.

Fighting for the Prize

The riches on board are thought to be worth between $4 billion and $17 billion in today's money. There were chests of emeralds and tons of silver, gold, and platinum. Many expeditions have set off in search of the wreck, determined to find its exact location and bring back the prize. Then, in 2015, the government of Colombia announced to the world that the mystery has been solved. A wreck had been found off the Colombian coast, near the city of Cartagena.

Immediately, the story caused arguments. A company that said it had located the wreck first, back in 1981, claimed to own a share of whatever treasure is discovered. The Colombian government said that the ship was found some way from the location that company gave, so the company did not have a claim. The government said that the treasure belongs to the Colombian nation. The conflict is certain to continue, but what does seem certain is that this fantastic wreck has finally been found. Surely it is only a matter of time before we see its riches once more?

Could the lost hoard of treasure really have been found?

MYSTERY HUNTER

Considering what you have learned about shipwrecks, do you think the wreck of the *Flor do Mar* is likely to be found? Back up your answer with evidence you have read in this chapter.

Chapter 6

BURIED TREASURE, BUT WHERE?

It is natural for people who amass a store of treasure to want to keep hold of it. After all, it may have taken a lifetime's effort to collect it, whether by fair means or foul. Sometimes, however, people have been so desperate to keep their riches safe that they have buried them somewhere secret, then died without passing on the secret of their location. Other hoards have simply been mislaid!

King John's Treasure

In 1216, in England, King John I (1166–1216) was traveling with the beautiful crown jewels he had inherited from his grandmother. The king fell sick, and although he took a safe route home to London by sea, he left his men to travel across land, along with all the baggage. The route they chose led them through coastal marshes, where the men became trapped by the tide. They all drowned, and the carts loaded with treasure sank with them. This priceless hoard has never been found.

King John I of England lost his priceless crown jewels.

Paul Kruger is shown on the South African krugerrand coin, which also takes his name.

Boer Gold

In the 1890s, the British were fighting a war with the Boers in South Africa. The Boers were the descendants of the Dutch people who had settled there. As the British advanced, the Boer president, Paul Kruger (1825–1904), fled toward the coast with a massive amount of treasure. There was gold from South Africa's banks and mines, and thousands of coins. Kruger escaped by sea but the treasure was left behind, somewhere in the countryside. Again, it has never been found.

MYSTERIOUS FACTS

Here are some major treasure hoards collected, and lost, during wartime:

- Millions of dollars of gold was lost at the end of the Civil War (1861–1865). It was hidden by the defeated Confederates to prevent the soldiers of the Union finding it.
- There is a story that during World War II (1939–1945), the German Nazis filled three trains with gold and other treasure that they had stolen from people, and hid them in railroad tunnels somewhere in Poland. Two men recently claimed to have found the location. However, in 2016, this claim was proven false.

In the Great Depression, people who lost their jobs and businesses took to the streets to protest.

Trabuco's Plan

In the early 1930s, the United States was in the middle of the Great Depression, an **economic** slump that brought poverty and unemployment to millions of people. Leon Trabuco was a Mexican millionaire. He was a successful businessman with a good eye for a moneymaking scheme. His final enterprise, however, ended in disaster. It also left a mystery that has never been solved.

Safety in Gold

In difficult economic times, the price of gold usually rises, because it is a safe thing in which to **invest**. Trabuco thought that the price of gold in the United States was bound to rise rapidly, so he and his partners started buying up large amounts of gold in Mexico. The idea was to sell it in the United States, and make a huge profit. It is said that Trabuco gathered more than 16 tons (14.5 t) of gold.

No Records

A plane like this one flew into the desert with secret cargoes of solid gold bars.

In 1933, Trabuco smuggled his gold illegally into the United States. To keep it safe, he hid it in the New Mexico desert. He hired a pilot named Red Moiser, who made 16 flights to the desert with the gold. Trucks then took it to its burial site. Trabuco was right. The price of gold in the United States did rise, but Trabuco was greedy. He decided to wait for the price to rise even farther before selling his hoard. This was his undoing. In 1934, the U.S. government passed a new law making it illegal for any private individual to own gold. There was now no way Trabuco could sell his treasure.

Trabuco never told anyone of the gold's location, and never made a map. When he died, he took the secret of its location to the grave. This treasure seemed also to carry a curse, as three of Trabuco's partners died mysteriously within five years. One treasure hunter spent decades looking for this gold. He believed he had identified a likely area, but died before he found the stash. Some say it was found long ago and the U.S. government secretly removed it; others say that it is still waiting to be found, somewhere in the desert.

The New Mexico desert is a vast area to search.

Lost Treasure of Lima

After the Spanish conquered Peru in the sixteenth century, they stole a huge amount of gold and other treasure from the wealthy empire of the local Inca people. The Spanish shipped loads of treasure back to their king in Spain. Over the next few centuries, they continued to collect quantities of gold and precious gems, which they stored in the Peruvian city of Lima. Eventually, in the early nineteenth century, Peruvians began to fight for their independence from Spain. What would happen to the treasure in Lima now?

A Bad Captain

The story goes that, in 1820, as the Peruvian army approached Lima, the Spanish decided to move their treasure to Mexico for safety. Unwisely, they gave it to a Canadian sea captain named William Thompson to look after. Instead of waiting with the treasure in the harbor, Thompson and his men killed the guards and sailed off with the treasure.

General José de San Martín proclaimed the independence of Peru in 1821.

They landed on Cocos Island, off the coast of Costa Rica, where they apparently buried the treasure. This was a real treasure island! Thompson and his men decided to lie low and come back for their treasure later. Unluckily for them, their ship was captured by the Spanish, they were put on trial, and most were killed. Thompson promised to take the Spanish to their treasure if they would spare his life. They did, but on Cocos Island he escaped into the jungle. He was never seen again.

Treasure Hunt

Since then, hundreds of people have searched Cocos Island for the treasure. A German man named August Gissler lived on the island from 1889 to 1908. He searched constantly, but found just six gold coins in that time. The search goes on. One theory is that Thompson did make his way back to the hoard and removed it. He joined a whaling ship and sailed to Canada. Another is that he misled the Spanish by taking them to Cocos Island, and had buried the treasure somewhere else.

Much of the lost treasure was religious artifacts belonging to the Catholic Church.

Crusaders do battle with Muslim soldiers during the First Crusade.

Lost Treasure of the Knights Templar

The Knights Templar was a group of Christian knights who gathered together in AD 1114 to fight in the Crusades. The Crusades were a series of expeditions from the eleventh to the thirteenth centuries that set off from Europe to the **Holy Land** to capture the city of Jerusalem from the Muslims who then ruled it. The Knights Templar set up headquarters in Jerusalem, and were declared a charity by the Pope. For 170 years, gifts of gold, silver, jewels, land, and castles from their supporters made them extremely wealthy. After Muslims took back control of the Holy Land, the knights fell out of favor. The Pope accused them of **heresy**, or religious practices not acceptable to the Church. He ordered them all to be arrested. Many of the knights escaped, taking their great riches with them. Where did they go?

In the 1930s, these excavations on Oak Island did not find any treasure. But several people were hurt.

A Bottomless Pit

The story goes that the knights took their treasure to Scotland, and later to Nova Scotia in Canada. The fate of the treasure centers on Oak Island, off the coast of Nova Scotia. In 1795, two men discovered a mysterious pit there. Beneath the surface were large flat stones. Digging down, they found a platform of logs every 9 feet (3 m) or so.

On one stone, there were symbols that some treasure hunters have translated as meaning: "Forty feet below, two million pounds lie buried." Since then, many, many attempts have been made to excavate the pit. No one has ever reached the bottom, as the dangerous hole floods with water. Several people have been hurt or killed in their attempts to reach the supposed treasure.

Mystery Hunters at the Ready

Stories of lost tombs and treasures will always dazzle people. The role of the mystery hunter is to examine these stories to discover the truth, weighing up the facts and gathering the scientific and historical evidence. The mystery hunter can also question why stories of curses are often linked with treasure. Whether curses are real or not, many people have died in their attempts to grasp riches beyond our wildest dreams.

MYSTERY HUNTER

Do you think the lost treasures of Leon Trabuco or of the Knights Templar will ever be found? Do they even exist? Give reasons for your answers.

MYSTERY HUNTER ANSWERS

Chapter 1

Q *Considering the information you have read, do you think that Atahualpa's treasure is still hidden somewhere? Could it have survived all this time without anyone finding it? Would the Inca have buried it out of sight? Give reasons for your answers.*

A It is possible that Atahualpa's gold is still buried in the mountains of Ecuador, or perhaps somewhere else entirely. There are records of several people finding it, but mysteriously they never survived to describe its location. It is also possible that the Inca shared the treasure after Atahualpa was killed. It will certainly be exciting to explore the recent find in the jungle, even if it does not contain any treasure.

Chapter 2

Q *Considering what you have read in this chapter, do you think the "Curse of the Pharaohs" really exists? Give reasons for your answer.*

A There was no curse written on Tutankhamun's tomb, and curse inscriptions on Egyptian tombs are actually quite rare. The legend of the curse was widely talked about only after 1922. Many of Howard Carter's team did meet with early deaths. However, Howard Carter himself died of natural causes a full 17 years later. Perhaps the "curse" is no more than a series of unfortunate coincidences.

Chapter 3

Q *Do you think it will ever be possible to unlock the secrets of Qin Shi Huang's tomb? Are the traps of weapons and poisons laid by this cunning emperor enough to keep us out forever? Justify your answers with information you have read in this chapter.*

A It is certainly a great challenge to open up the tomb of Qin Shi Huang. There is no reason to believe that the crossbows set up to fire arrows at intruders are not still working perfectly! The risk of mercury pollution to the surrounding area is also high. However, today we have sophisticated technologies that can create images of the interior of the tomb without even opening it, so let us hope that one day we will see all the splendors of this historic site.

Chapter 4

Q *Based on what you have read about Gilgamesh and the city of Uruk, do you think archaeologists have discovered the burial place of Gilgamesh in Iraq? Give reasons for your answer.*

A The location of the structure in the ancient riverbed does match the location of Gilgamesh's tomb described in the story. However, for some, Gilgamesh's story is just that: a story. Others are sure that Gilgamesh really lived and that his tomb must exist. It is possible Gilgamesh is buried in Uruk, but only more exploration can reveal the truth.

Chapter 5

Q *Considering what you have learned about shipwrecks, do you think the wreck of the* Flor do Mar *is likely to be found? Back up your answer with evidence you have read in this chapter.*

A Even using modern technology such as sonar, this amazing wreck may never be found. The ship sank in an area of strong currents, so it was probably broken up and its pieces quickly scattered over a wide area. Its treasures have probably sunk far into the seabed, if they were not stolen immediately by local people.

Chapter 6

Q *Do you think the lost treasures of Leon Trabuco or of the Knights Templar will ever be found? Do they even exist? Give reasons for your answers.*

A It seems very unlikely that either of these treasure hoards will ever come to light. The desert of New Mexico is a huge place to search, even if the gold was not removed decades ago. The treasure of the Knights Templar is only one suggestion of what might be lying at the bottom of the pit on Oak Island, but it seems to be impossible to get to the bottom of this mystery, quite literally!

GLOSSARY

afterlife life after death

amassed gathered together

archaeologists people who study the past by digging for the remains of buildings and objects

artifacts objects made by people in the past

cargo goods carried by ships

chambers rooms

colonies areas of land controlled by a foreign power

complex a collection of buildings

conquistador a Spanish or Portuguese soldier or explorer who, from the sixteenth century, invaded and took over lands in the Americas

corroded eaten away over time

culture the customs and arts of a people

cuneiform a system of writing using wedge-shaped characters

currents large movements in a body of water

custom the usual way of behaving or doing something

dynasty a ruling family

economic concerned with money, trade, and the way money is spent

empire a collection of lands ruled by one country

evidence objects or information that prove something is true

excavated dug up

galleon a large sailing ship

heresy a belief that disagrees with the beliefs of the Christian Church

hieroglyphic related to a system of writing that uses pictures as symbols

hoards large collections

Holy Land a region centered on modern Israel and Palestine, containing places holy to Christians, Jews, and Muslims

inscriptions words that are carved into a hard surface, such as stone

intact in one piece; not destroyed

invest to put money into something in the hopes of making a profit

legacy something passed down from a person or group of people to others

legends old stories that may or may not be true

nomadic describes people who move from one place to another to live

pavilion a building in a garden or park

pharaohs rulers of ancient Egypt

philosopher a person who studies the truths about life

probes instruments used to carry out close examinations

quarry a place from which raw materials are dug from the ground

quests lengthy searches

radar a system of using radio waves to show the locations of things

sacred holy

thermal to do with heat

vault an underground chamber

ziggurats tall pyramids with stepped sides and flat tops

FOR MORE INFORMATION

BOOKS

Barber, Nicola. *Lost Cities* (Treasure Hunters). North Mankato, MN: Raintree, 2013.

Caldwell, Stella. *Explore 360° The Tomb of Tutankhamun*. Hauppauge, NY: Barron's Educational Series, 2016.

Jameson, W.C. *Buried Treasures of the Pacific Northwest.* Atlanta, GA: August House, 2006.

O'Brien, Cynthia. *Lost Treasures* (Mystery Files). New York, NY: Crabtree, 2015.

WEBSITES

Learn more about ancient Egypt at:
www.ducksters.com/history/ancient_egypt.php

Do some research about ancient civilizations and their great men and women at:
www.history.com/topics/ancient-history

Explore this site about lost underwater treasures:
www.oceantreasures.org

Find out all about archaeology at:
www.q-files.com/history/archaeology/archaeology

Publisher's note to educators and parents: Our editors have carefully reviewed these websites to ensure that they are suitable for students. Many websites change frequently, however, and we cannot guarantee that a site's future contents will continue to meet our high standards of quality and educational value. Be advised that students should be closely supervised whenever they access the Internet.

INDEX